"Smith shows us how to grow ho, . . joy in our homes. Full of fresh, engaging, and helpful prompts and ideas, this book is a gift!" – **Jennifer Grant, author of *A Little Blue Bottle* and *Maybe God Is Like That Too***

"The gift of Traci Smith's new book is that you can open it anywhere and find one simple, lovely thing to do, pray, tell, or make with your family that day (or let's be honest, as Traci is, maybe the next day) to add joy and meaning to the holiday season. Advent is a time to draw near to God as God draws near to us in the birth of Jesus, and *Faithful Families for Advent & Christmas* is brimming over with wonderful, easy suggestions to help you do just that." —**Wendy Claire Barrie, author of *Faith at Home: A Handbook for Cautiously Christian Parents***

"The beautiful thing about this book is that even though a plethora of Advent, Christmas, and Epiphany practices are presented, author Traci Smith does not overwhelm families, but instead manages to encourage them to celebrate sacred moments and find together the true meaning of this holy season. This book truly is a treasure." —**Glenys Nellist, author of *'Twas The Evening of Christmas* and *'Twas The Season of Advent***

"Traci creatively turns all kinds of simple acts into opportunities for both sweet and profound connection." —**Arianne Braithwaite Lehn, author of *Ash and Starlight: Prayers for the Chaos and Grace of Life***

"Can you have too much of a good thing? Not if you're talking about Traci Smith's creative ideas for infusing faith into daily life. This book is a gift to all who want to enrich the spiritual lives of families as they celebrate Advent and Christmas with one another. Within these pages are rich insights, honest prayers, and compelling practices. Unwrap them with your family and enliven the spirit and the spiritual of the holidays." —**David M. Csinos, Atlantic School of Theology and Founder of Faith Forward**

"As promised, far from taxing families with MORE to do during hectic Advent and Christmas seasons, Rev. Traci Smith offers families what we really need: LESS to do. In each of these simple, hands-on practices, Smith gives families the tools to slow down, wait, and focus on all that Jesus coming into the world means. This is a must-have for any family or children's ministry leader's library." —**Caryn Rivadeneira, author of *Grit and Grace: Heroic Women of the Bible***

"Christmas can be overwhelming, and the faith we affirm can get lost in the shuffle. *Faithful Families for Advent & Christmas* will help families claim their home as a sanctuary from the overwhelming rush of Christmas. Families will also find everything they need to prepare for and celebrate Christmas. Families of all sizes and ages will find ideas to deepen their faith and grow closer to each other." —**Lee Yates, Project Manager for *InsideOut* Outdoor Ministries Resources**

100 WAYS TO MAKE THE SEASON SACRED

FAITHFUL FAMILIES

FOR ADVENT & CHRISTMAS

A holiday companion to *Faithful Families: Creating Sacred Moments at Home*

TRACI SMITH

chalice
press

Saint Louis, Missouri

An imprint of Christian Board of Publication

Bible quotations, unless otherwise noted, are from the *New Revised Standard Version Bible,* copyright 1989, Division of Christian Education of the National Council of the Churches of Christ in the United States of America. Used by permission. All rights reserved.

Cover design and art: Paul Soupiset
Interior design: Connie H.C. Wang

ChalicePress.com

PRINT: 9780827211360
EPUB: 9780827211377
EPDF: 9780827211384

Printed in the United States of America

For Samuel, Marina Lynn, and Clayton

With love, Mom

Contents

OPENING WORDS

I don't know who first said that parenting comprises "long days and short years," but I have found this to be a powerful truth in my experience as a parent. Sometimes there is a daily grind of grubby fingers, skinned knees, peanut butter sandwiches, and piles of dishes. And then, out of nowhere... poof! My child is nine years old. How did that happen when, just yesterday, he was learning to walk on his own two feet? All those mothers who told me "it goes by so fast" were telling me the truth, even though I didn't believe it.

As a writer who focuses on connecting faith to practice, particularly for families, I am mindful that one of the remedies for making the long days count is a deliberate focus on ritual to mark the moments. It doesn't take long, just a few minutes in the midst of ordinary life to slow down, and say "this day will not pass by unnoticed."

There are way more ideas in this book than you need. Just pick out a few of them and your work is done. Don't worry about everything being perfect or tidy; the effort you make is everything. As you try to make meaning in the everyday, I think you'll find the Spirit is present right there with you in the middle of all the messiness, just waiting to show you something surprising. Holy moments are a gift. Sometimes the more we force them, the less they appear. So don't worry about trying to "do" the activities in this book. Focus instead on letting them come naturally to you, at just the right moment. You'll know what to do.

The Faithful Families Perspective on Advent and Christmas

What Is Advent?

In the church's calendar (called the liturgical calendar), Advent is the four weeks prior to Christmas. In the church year, Advent starts on a Sunday, four weeks before Christmas. This means, depending on how the days of the week fall, Advent begins in the final days of November or the first days of December. When it comes to celebrating Advent at home, I'm not so sure it's important to identify Advent precisely with the first Sunday of Advent, though we certainly may. We may also choose to begin our Advent practice the day after Thanksgiving or, perhaps, on the first of December. No matter which exact day your family celebration of Advent begins, let it be the beginning of a time of individual and family growth. For Christians, Advent is a time of preparation and waiting. We prepare our hearts and our lives for the birth of the baby Jesus. In this time of waiting, we can embark on spiritual practices that help center us and prepare for this day. Advent is a time of great opportunity and expectation, a time to slow down, rest, and prepare.

What Is Christmas?

Though we often think of Christmas in terms of a single day, December 25, the liturgical (church) celebration of Christmas is much more than that. It's a season. Starting on December 25, the day Jesus is born, and ending on

January 6, the celebration of the day the Magi came to bring gifts to Jesus, the season of Christmas is a joyful time to celebrate all that Christ's birth means in our lives.

The messages our culture throws at us at Advent and Christmas are loud and clear: Buy. Run. Decorate. Be busy. Most of all...*be perfect.* The pressure can be enormous to have *just the right gift* or *the perfect family gathering.* No family is perfect. No holiday season can be perfect either. The prayers, practices, and stories in this book are designed to be a breath of fresh air for you during the season. Let them encourage you to seek out the Advent values of hope, peace, joy, and love with your family. Rather than adding on one more thing to do, use the ideas as a way to say no to the hustle and bustle of consumerism and perfectionism. Spend time with your family. Connect. Say a prayer. Do something together. You won't regret it. As you incorporate some of the practices in this book throughout your Advent and Christmas season, you will find the season taking on layers of spiritual meaning beyond the twinkling lights and wrapped packages. With practice, Advent and Christmas can be one of the holiest times of the year. The reward for your children is great, too: Their Advent and Christmas inheritance is one of faith, family, and holy moments.

There are 100 total prayers, practices, and stories in this book. It would be over the top to attempt to do all 100 in a single Advent and Christmas season. The book isn't designed that way. Instead, it's designed for you to read through at your leisure and try various practices as time and interest allow. It's also been my experience that when families try prayers, practices, and lessons like the ones in this book, not every single one will resonate. Maybe a family member will complain or refuse to participate. Something might make a huge mess. Not all of the attempts will be wins, but the attempt and the consistency are what matter. When you find something that works well for your family, repeat it. Let it become tradition. Maybe you'll have to redefine your idea of success for the purposes of some of these exercises. If everyone gets together and gives one of the practices a solid attempt, consider that a win. I encourage families to try a practice at least twice before giving up on it. Eventually you'll find a practice or a prayer that sticks for your family. You'll recognize it when it happens. When you find a practice that seems just right for your family, incorporate it into the fabric of your family life and pass it on for generations to come. Sometimes I talk about the spiritual practices I write about as recipes. Some people like to follow the recipe exactly, and others use it as a guide, adding a dash of this or that to make it their own. I've done my best to provide the structure for you, but I hope you'll want to take these ideas and make them truly your own.

With regard to the prayers in this book, I hope you'll find them to be unexpected and unique. Some are designed to teach about breath prayer. Some are more meditative, or affirmation-like. The intention here is, again, to inspire you. Feel free to pray the prayers as they are with your family, but also let them inspire you to write your own prayers, knowing that God loves to be in conversation with us. More than anything, I hope the prayers in this book are a reminder that there's no one "right way to pray." Children express their prayers through movement and wiggles just as often as they do through bowed heads and folded hands. Prayers can be written, spoken, or felt in the heart. Don't be afraid to experiment and play with your prayers.

Notes for Parents and Guardians

On Letting Things Go and the Tradeoffs

Our time is finite. When we choose what we're going to do, we are, by definition, choosing *not* to do other things. A decision to spend time with family is a decision not to spend that time working, cleaning, shopping, or attending holiday gatherings. As much as we'd like to think we can do it all, we can't. The practices in this book are an invitation to make a conscious choice to choose time with your family *instead of* some of the other things. If you approach this book as another list of things to do on top of an already full and busy life, you'll make yourself crazy. Choose, instead, to say no to some of the other things the season has to offer. Some families might find it useful to cut out entire categories of to-dos in order to make room for family. "No baking from scratch" was one of my guidelines one year at Christmas. Somehow it gave me great freedom to take it off the table completely in a way that "I'll bake less this year" would not have. The same goes for accepting invitations. Telling others that your family has decided to decline all invitations helps to create an even playing field and make rejections less personal.

Creating a Sacred Space

In some of my other writing, I advocate for creating a sacred space in your home where family members can go to rest and encounter the Holy Spirit. If you have the space, perhaps a corner or closet can be transformed with soft pillows and lighting to become a sacred space for your family to gather, either individually or as a group. For Christmastime, light up the space with white lights or other Christmas decorations. Another idea for a sacred space is to have a small altar, or perhaps a table with a nativity scene or prayer basket. Whether your sacred space is large or tiny, let it be a place of rest and renewal for your family.

Finding Rest as a Parent

As a minister, my colleagues are often reminding me that I can't pour out for others that which I don't have myself. One cannot drink from an empty well. The same is true for parents and children. If you'd like to create sacred and holy moments for your family, you must first start from a place of peace and balance within yourself. It is not selfish, as a parent, to take time for rest and renewal for yourself before embarking on a time of creating something special for your children and family. If you're exhausted, rest. If you need to seek counsel or healing within yourself, do that first before trying to create a perfect space for your family or children. If this is not the year to do the practices in this book, set it aside. It will be here next year. Take care of yourself, first and foremost, that you might have an abundance to share with your family.

Being Gentle When Things Don't Go Perfectly

One constant in family life: Things rarely go as planned. I've embarked on many a family activity, project, or faith moment with my children only to have things end up straying quite far from the original plan. Sometimes children don't want to participate, get the wiggles, or act out. Sometimes I find I'm much grumpier than I thought I was and am impatient with the moment. Sometimes we have to just let it go. And then, there are times when a sacred moment just sort of appears, seemingly out of nowhere. I cherish those moments! I think it's wise to approach the practices in this book with a sense of lightness. Don't hold on too tightly to them. Expect that some will bomb and that others might surprise you. It's unrealistic to think that every family moment will be a smashing success. Families are messy, and sometimes there's beauty in that holy mess. Try to laugh it off when things don't go as planned: "Well *that* was something! We can try again tomorrow."

A Word on Repetition

I think the beauty in these practices comes in the repetition. Plowing through every practice in this book is probably not as effective as picking a few practices and repeating them weekly or (in the case of some of the prayers) daily. Picking a practice or two and repeating it annually over many years is also a powerful way to create lasting memories. Choose quality over quantity, repetition over novelty.

Where to Store the Book

I suggest storing this book not on a bookshelf but in the same boxes where you store your Christmas decorations. That way, it'll be waiting for you each year as a special treat when you start the Advent season. Otherwise, it might get lost among other non-seasonal books and not make its way out into the fore when Advent rolls around. Give it a try!

A Note on Ages

Finding activities that are meaningful for family members of all ages can be a challenge. The practices in this book are designed for families with children of all ages. Faith is learned, not in one moment but as an accumulation of countless small moments. Often faith is learned through imitation and "copying." It's never too early to start some of these practices, even if children seem to be too young. They'll be learning by watching and learning. Here are some specific tips for children at the younger and older ends of the spectrum.

Tips for Younger Children

- Remember attention spans. For the littlest ones, two to three minutes is plenty of time.
- Adjust your expectations. If you don't get through the whole practice or prayer, that's okay. Do what you can, and remember that the goal is to spend time together.

- Ask young children to repeat the words of prayers after an adult says them, one line at a time.

- Where the practices call for writing something down, have young children draw pictures instead.

- Ask open-ended questions. Statements beginning with "I wonder..." are also a great way to invite young children into the stories. (For example, "I wonder what it was like on that night when Jesus was born...")

Tips for Older Children and Teens

- Give choices. Give the book to them and let them choose a practice or prayer that speaks to them.

- Ask them to lead. Maybe older children and teens will choose to do a practice in a different way or put their own spin on it. Some older children might prefer helping younger ones in the family with the activities if they feel too elementary for them.

- Invite questions and comments. "What do you think about this story?"

- I encourage families to invite participation rather than require it.

Notes for Ministry Leaders

I have the utmost respect for those ministry leaders who are called to lead family ministries with children. One of the challenging parts of the job is balancing the needs of all of the people with whom you work: parents, children, families, volunteers, and coworkers. This resource is for families, but my hope is that ministry leaders will use it as well. More importantly, you are able to model how to use these resources for the families in your care.

Giving Parents a Place to Rest—Freedom from Perfection

I don't know many parents who never question whether or not they're doing it right. In fact, most of the parents I know find themselves constantly questioning their parenting. When it comes to nurturing a healthy spirituality with children, things become even more challenging. Some parents question whether or not they have enough knowledge to teach their children, preferring to leave that teaching to church educators and pastors. As a ministry leader, it's up to you to encourage the parents in your care and remind them that perfection is not the aim. God is pleased with our wholehearted attempts to share the gifts we have been given with our children. Help your people laugh when things go amusingly astray, and celebrate the smallest of successes.

Modeling That Less Is More

If you gift this book to the families in your congregation, be sure to emphasize that there's an entire buffet of options here and that there's no need to choose more than a few. You can act as curator and choose the practices you think work well with the messages you're emphasizing in your congregation and ministry. Perhaps you'll choose a practice or two per week and highlight it for your congregation.

Teaching These Practices as a Group and Having Families Practice Them at Home

There's something comforting and helpful in knowing that we're not alone as we try new things with our families. Use your influence as a ministry leader to teach families these practices and keep them accountable (in a fun way) to doing them. Have a "prayer of the week" that you teach during your time together, and then ask families to pray it together during the week. Do the same with the practices. You could also empower families to do some of the activities by getting the materials ready for them and directing them to the appropriate page or practice.

Finding Rest as a Ministry Leader

Whenever I write for families, I have ministry leaders in mind as well. How can you use the practices in this book to make life easier for yourself? Perhaps one of the practices works well as a children's message or as a devotional for you. Maybe it kickstarts your imagination and leads you to an activity you'd like to do with your families in a workshop or teaching moment. Rest is important for you, too.

Honoring That Times Can Be Difficult

One of the things I've tried to build into *Faithful Families for Advent and Christmas* is an acknowledgement that things aren't only rosy at Advent and Christmas. Times can be challenging and difficult. As a ministry leader, you can model this by lifting up some of the prayers for difficult times. You can hold space for people who are grieving or sad, overwhelmed or tired during this season. These practices are here to help you.

Permissions

The prayers, practices, and lessons in this book are designed to be shared and modified as you see fit. Use the lessons as a jumping-off place for a children's message or a moment of focus and centering at the beginning of a church potluck. Teach one of the prayers to everyone during an education hour or during worship. Print out a practice for your families to take home and try during the week.

You are permitted to excerpt up to five prayers, practices, and lessons from this book in your church communications (social media posts, newsletter, bulletin, etc.). When you do, please use the following attribution: "Excerpted from *Faithful Families for Advent and Christmas: 100 Prayers, Practices, and Lessons to Make the Season Sacred* by Traci Smith (Chalice Press: 2020, All Rights Reserved)."

Chapter 1: Beginnings

The four weeks leading up to Christmas Day are called Advent, from the Latin *adventus,* meaning "coming" or "arrival." It is a season of waiting and preparation before the birth of Jesus, a time to prepare our hearts and our homes for the arrival of the baby Jesus. This time of waiting invites us to take time to slow down and reflect instead of diving in headfirst to all of the glitz and glitter. That we must wait for Christ to be born is a spiritual discipline and a useful practice. We live in a society that tells us we can have what we want instantly. The message of Advent challenges this and invites us into a time of deliberate waiting, though this is not the message we receive from the culture around us. The cultural expectations of the season to spend, to entertain, and to hurry are in stark opposition to the spiritual invitation of the season, which is to wait, to reflect, and to slow down.

The practices and prayers in this chapter invite you and your family to observe a holy Advent, rooted in waiting and preparation. The practices laid out here are not meant to add another "to-do" in the midst of an already crowded season. On the contrary, this chapter is an invitation for you to plan your Advent season around moments of connection and meaning before things get too hectic. Perfection is not the goal. How will you create holy space in your home and life this season? The practices that follow will help you answer this question.

Spiritual Practices
for Beginning the Season

Set an Advent Intention

Spiritual practice is not just "accidental." If your Advent season is to be a time when connection, family time, and spiritual practice are the focus, it will happen because you and your family have made it a priority. This is not easy, and it goes against the tide of culture. Before the hustle and bustle of the season, take a few moments to set an Advent intention. What would you like the season to look like? Would you like to intentionally limit the number of outside invitations you accept as a family in order to have more peace and less rush? Would you like to set aside one day of the week for family time? Maybe you would like to be guided by an Advent word such as *peace, joy, hope,* or *love*. Get the whole family in on the discussion, as age and maturity level allow. If you choose, write down your intention in a journal or somewhere the whole family can see it. The Advent intention will look different for each family, but here are a few examples:

- This Advent, we will focus on the Advent values of hope, peace, love, and joy.

- We will not be overscheduled this Advent, but instead, we will take time for one another.

- Every Sunday evening during Advent, we will do a spiritual practice together.

- Advent will be a time of peace and quiet for our family, not noise and hustle.

Create a Sacred Space

Advent and Christmas are a time for decorating and making space. As you prepare your home for Christmas, consider setting apart a sacred space that will be devoted to some of the prayers and practices in this book. The sacred space can be as simple as a small table. Place this book on the table with perhaps some of the prayers in it written on separate slips of paper, an Advent calendar, or any of the other symbols you create as you work through the practices of this book. Perhaps you will add some candles or sacred objects from your own family. However you create the space, your family will know that it is set apart for spiritual practice. If you have the space, add a chair where family members can come and sit for a few minutes of peace and quiet during the season.

Make a "Not-to-Do" List

Often, we busy ourselves with endless "to-do" lists, especially during a busy season such as Advent. One fun way to turn off worry and the tendency to achieve and to do is to make a "not-to-do" list. What are the things you and your family want to be intentional about *not* doing this Advent season? Maybe your not-to-do list will include "spend too much time shopping," or "worry," or "schedule." Consider what takes away from your spiritual health and well-being, and put it on the list. The not-to-do list could be done individually or as a family. If you decide to do it as a family, you could do one collaborative list or have each person make their own list and then compare when you're done. Approach this exercise with levity and fun. Sometimes the best way to figure out what we want to do is to define what we *don't* want to do. The not-to-do list need not be long. Perhaps it is simply one or two things you vow to let go of this season. End your not-to-do list session with a quick reminder that God is with us throughout the season, no matter what we do (or don't do!). Pray: *God, thank you for all of the possibilities this season of Advent and Christmas brings. Help us to let go of the things that aren't important and focus on your Spirit. Amen.*

Acts of Kindness Advent Tree

This Advent calendar is created by adding acts of kindness on a tree as they are completed. Here's how to make it:

Step 1: Find a branch from outside and put it in a vase.

Step 2: Write down acts of kindness (see below for examples) on paper ornaments and place them in a basket.

Step 3: As you complete each act of kindness throughout the Advent season, punch a hole in the ornament and tie it to your acts of kindness tree.

Variations:

- Put the acts of kindness ornaments on your Christmas tree instead of a separate branch.

- Write acts of kindness on a sheet of paper and put a star next to them as they are completed.

Ten Acts of Kindness for an Acts of Kindness Advent Tree

1. Hold the door open for someone at the store.

2. Return grocery carts in a parking lot.

3. Bake sweet treats and take them to a neighbor.

4. Help a family member or friend put up Christmas lights or decorate their house.

5. Leave a kind note on someone's windshield.

6. Write a thank-you note to someone who serves you.

7. Collect mittens and hats for a local charity.

8. Pick up trash in your neighborhood or local park.

9. Bring dog or cat food to a pet shelter.

10. Color paper placemats and take them to a senior center.

Paper Chain Advent Calendar

An Advent calendar marks the days until Christmas, and a paper chain calendar is one of the simplest styles. Simply take 24 (or 25) strips of paper and link them together, removing one each day until Christmas. The chain is a visual reminder of how many days are left until Christmas. There are endless variations on a paper chain Advent calendar. Here are some ideas to get you started:

• Number the strips as you put them together.

• Color Christmas symbols and scenes on the strips.

• Write down ideas for fun things you will do together and then do them as you remove them from the chain.

• Make an Advent chain in reverse: Instead of removing a link from the chain each day, start with one link and add a link every day. Each day you add to the chain, write down something you are grateful for on the link, or write down a memory from the day. At the end of Advent, you'll have a chain full of gratitude or memories!

Jesse Tree

A Jesse tree is a tree of symbols that tell the story of Jesus, beginning all the way at the beginning of the Bible in the book of Genesis. The name "Jesse Tree" comes from a prophesy in the book of Isaiah that says, "A shoot shall come out from the stump of Jesse, and a branch shall grow out of his roots. The spirit of the LORD shall rest on him, the spirit of wisdom and understanding, the spirit of counsel and might, the spirit of knowledge and the fear of the LORD. His delight shall be in the fear of the LORD" (Isaiah 11:1–3). Christians have long understood this passage to be a prophesy about Jesus.

A Jesse tree usually has 25 symbols and 25 stories. Each story is told with a symbol on one side and a reading on the other side. Make your own ornaments, or look for a Jesse tree pattern on the internet. There are many variations to make or buy.

Another way to appreciate the Jesse tree is to do an online search of "Jesse tree stained glass window" images and pick out the symbols you can from the windows. There are many intricate and lovely designs. Print some out and look at the symbolism as a family.

Advent Wreath

Many Protestant and Roman Catholic churches use Advent wreaths to mark the passing of the four weeks in Advent. The candles are lit, one additional one per week, for four weeks. On Christmas Eve, a fifth candle is lit to represent Christ, the light of the world. In this version for the home, the family gathers around a very simple votive wreath to have dessert together and reflect on each of the four Advent values: hope, peace, joy, and love.

To make your wreath, place four votive candles on a plate in a circle with a pillar candle in the center. Light one candle per week, starting with the first Sunday in Advent (four weeks before Christmas). On each subsequent week, light an additional candle. The first week represents hope; the second, peace; the third, joy; and the fourth, love. On Christmas Eve, light all four candles as well as the candle in the middle, representing the baby Jesus.

During each of the four weeks of Advent, on Sunday evening after dinner, sit around the table with your dessert and candles and go through the simple routine of lighting the candle, discussing the Advent value, and ending with a simple prayer. The depth of discussion will vary, depending on the ages of children involved. For very young children, simply saying the word and ending with the prayer is sufficient and lays the foundation for future years. For more in-depth discussion of each of the values, you may choose to lean on some of the practices in chapter 6.

Week 1: Hope

Light: Today we light the candle of hope.

Read (optional): Psalm 25:4–5

Discuss: What does it mean to have hope? What do you think about when you hear the word *hope*? How can we share hope with others?

Pray: *God, we thank you for giving us hope. Help us to have hope and to share hope as we wait for Jesus to be born. Amen.*

Week 2: Peace

Light: Today we light the candle of hope and the candle of peace.

Read (optional): John 14:25–27

Discuss: What does it mean to have peace in your heart? How can we share peace in our family and in the world?

Pray: *God, please help us to understand peace and to share it with others. We wait for Jesus to be born with hope and peace. Amen.*

Week 3: Joy

Light: Today we light the candles of hope, peace, and joy.

Read (optional): Philippians 4:4–6

Discuss: What does it mean to rejoice? How is joy the same or different from happiness? How can we share joy with others?

Pray: *God, we thank you for the gift of joy. Help us to share it with one another. We wait for Jesus with hope, peace, and joy. Amen.*

Week 4: Love

Light: Today we light the candles of hope, peace, joy, and love.

Read (optional): 1 John 4:7–12

Discuss: When have you felt or seen God's love? How can we show God's love to the world?

Pray: *God, thank you for showing us what true love is. Help us to love you and to love one another. We wait for Jesus with hope, peace, joy, and love. Amen.*

Christmas Eve or Christmas Day: The Christ Candle

Light: Today we light the candles for hope, peace, joy, and love, and we light the center candle for the birth of Jesus.

Read (optional): Luke 2:1–16

Discuss: The day we have been waiting for is here! How does it feel to celebrate the birth of Jesus today? What does the birth of Jesus mean to you?

Pray: *God, today we are thankful for the birth of your son, Jesus, and for the lessons he teaches us about how to love one another. Help us throughout the year to share hope, peace, joy, and love wherever we go. Amen.*

Prayers
for Beginning the Season

A Prayer for Advent

As we wait for the birth of Jesus, we pause and think about what we want this season to be:

a season of hope,

a season of peace,

a season of joy,

a season of love,

a season of family togetherness,

a season of reflection.

At the Beginning of Advent

During Advent, we wait:

We wait for Christmas Day.

We wait to give and to receive.

We wait for family.

God, please help us to be patient as we wait

and to enjoy the journey together.

While We Wait for Christmas

While we wait for the excitement of Christmas Day, we pray for patience to enjoy the season with our family. May we always remember to be kind to one another, to spend time together, and to slow down when things get hectic. Help us as we share your love with others this season.

Chapter 2: Decorating

Getting the house ready with decorations can be a fun part of preparing for Christmas. This chapter guides you through some ways of making the chore of "decking the halls" a spiritual practice. These practices offer some basic ideas to which you can add your own touches, depending on your own family traditions. As you take out the decorations, for example, tell the stories of where they came from, who made them, or what they mean. Focus less on having a picture-perfect home and more on making your decorations meaningful. Since Advent is a time of waiting and preparation, there's no need to rush. Take your time, and prepare with intention and purpose.

Spiritual Practices for Decorating

Tell the Story of the Christmas Tree

When you put out your Christmas tree, take a moment to talk about the meaning and symbolism of the Christmas tree. People have been using green things from nature to decorate their homes for thousands of years. The ancient Egyptian people used palm branches, and ancient Roman people used evergreen branches. The green color reminded them of new life and new growth.

The tradition of decorating an evergreen tree at Christmastime is another way we use nature to decorate. German immigrants in Pennsylvania in the 1800s were the first people in the U.S. to use a tree at Christmastime as a symbol of the season.

Today, most Christians have a real or artificial tree in their houses at Christmastime. The tree is a great place to hang ornaments and pretty decorations, but it's also a symbol of something that stays green all year. It is *ever*green. In places where it freezes and ices and snows, the evergreen keeps its needles and green color all year long. When other branches are bare and empty, an evergreen's branches are lush and full.

The story is told that Martin Luther, a famous church reformer, was the first to tie candles to a green tree because it looked to him like stars twinkling through the green trees in the winter. When you see your green tree with lights, maybe it will remind you of some of the beautiful things in nature and the beauty that God created. When you see twinkling stars, maybe you will want to say, "Thank you, God, for the beauty you have made."

To talk about together: *What does your Christmas tree mean to you? Does it make you think of a real tree in nature?*

Tell the Story of the Poinsettia

If you buy, or are given, a poinsettia, take a moment to talk about the legend of the poinsettia. Poinsettias are the beautiful star-shaped red flowers that are associated with Christmas. An old Mexican legend tells how the flowers became associated with Christmas:

> Once upon a time, there was a little girl named Pepita who had no present to bring to the baby Jesus for Christmas Eve service. Her cousin, Pedro, reminded Pepita that even the smallest gifts can bring joy to the baby, and so Pepita brought a handful of weeds to the chapel. Suddenly, Pepita's offering turned into the bright red flowers we know as poinsettias. After that, the flowers were known as *las flores de la Nochebuena,* or "flowers of the Holy Night."

Whenever we see the red poinsettias, we can remember that our gifts are valuable to God.

To talk about together: *What gift do you have to bring to the baby Jesus? Maybe your gift is something tangible like flowers, but maybe it's something else, such as a talent.*

Tell the Story of the Candy Cane

When you see the shape of a candy cane, what do you think of? Many people say that a candy cane looks like a shepherd's crook. What does this mean for our faith? In the Bible, Jesus says, "I am the good shepherd" (John 10:11,). One of the tools a shepherd uses is a called a shepherd's crook, which is a long pole with a small curve at the end of it. The shepherd's crook is used to help keep the sheep safe. Using the crook, the shepherd can make sure the sheep are out of danger and going in the direction they need to go.

As you look at a candy cane, let it be a reminder to you that Jesus is like a good shepherd for us. When we listen to Jesus in prayer, we can have a sense of what is the right direction to go, away from danger and away from the things we believe are harmful or wrong.

To talk about together: *How is Jesus like a shepherd? What does that mean to you? When have you been guided away from danger?*

Find Yourself in the Nativity

This practice, like several practices in this book, uses a nativity scene as a place to begin reflection and discussion. If your nativity scene is not fragile and is easily moved to a place for discussion, bring it to the center of the table and ask family members to sit around and each take a piece. One family member will have Mary, another Joseph, and so on. Go around the table and talk about your character. What was your character's role in the birth of the baby Jesus? How did they feel? After everyone has a chance to talk and share their thoughts on their character, ask this question: *Where do you see yourself in the nativity?* Which character seemed the easiest to relate to? How would *you* feel if you found yourself in the nativity scene? What would it look like, smell like, and feel like there? Ask family members questions about what they're feeling and experiencing, too, and see what is similar and different from each person's perspective.

Make Luminaries

A luminary is simply an object that gives off light. Many people make luminaries to light the way to church or home on Christmas Eve. They are a beautiful addition to the sidewalk or driveway leading up to the door of the church or home. Traditional luminaries are made with paper bags. Designs are cut out of the bag, and tissue is affixed behind the cutouts. After the design is done, the bags are filled with a couple of inches of kitty litter or gravel, and candles are carefully placed inside. I strongly suggest using battery operated candles for your luminary. Though paper bag luminaries are the most traditional, there are many different options for making luminaries, from oranges to ice to clay. Do your research and choose the type of luminary that will be easiest for your family. As you light your luminary, remember Jesus's words, "I am the light of the world" (John 8:12), and ask, *How do we share our light with others?*

Prayers and Blessings
for Decorating

Christmas Tree Blessing*

God who created all things, bless this tree as we decorate it and make it a joyful symbol for our home. May its branches remind us of the shelter and shade you provide for us and for many creatures. May its trunk remind us of your strength. May its lights bring us peace. May we remember your gift to us this season, the gift of baby Jesus, Amen.

*This blessing is a paraphrase of one that was originally published in *Faithful Families: Creating Sacred Moments at Home* (St. Louis: Chalice Press, 2017).

Putting the Angel or Star on Top of the Tree

Angel:

As we put the angel on top of the tree, we remember the angels in the Bible who say, "Do not be afraid!" May we be reminded of the modern-day angels who tell us the same thing and who watch over us all night and all day.

Star:

The stars in the Bible shine light and show the way to Jesus. So, too, may this star shine brightly on our tree, reminding us that Jesus can light our path.

For Hanging Stockings

We hang up our stockings, empty, knowing that they'll later be filled with treats and treasures. May these stockings also remind us of the warmth of family, the joy of being with others, and the truest Christmas treasures of all: hope and peace, joy and love. Help us to share these treasures with others.

For Putting Out the Nativity

As we put out our nativity figures, one by one, we reflect on each:

Mary, and her bravery and strength; Joseph, and his compassion and loyalty; The baby Jesus, and his holiness and royalty. We add the other figures, too, as we find them: The shepherds watching over their flocks; The magi who will come to bring gifts of gold, frankincense, and myrrh; The angels who say, "Do not fear!" And the star who shines brightly, watching over all. God, please bless this nativity, and bless us as we use it to remember the story of Christ. Amen.

When We Decorate the Outside of Our Home

We thank you God for the blessing of a home to keep us warm and safe and dry. We decorate our house, today, to celebrate Advent and Christmas. May the lights shine bright and remind us of Christ's love.

Chapter 3: Family Time

Sometimes during a busy season such as Advent, we spend a lot of time *being together*, but not a lot of time *connecting* as a family. The practices in this chapter are designed to help your family grow together spiritually and to enjoy one another's company. Most are easy to do and don't take a lot of time, either. Commit to doing a few of the practices together during the season and enjoy the time of connection, fun, and spiritual growth.

Spiritual Practices
for Family Time

Christmas Card Prayers

Christmas card prayers is a practice I've seen in a lot of clergy groups, though I don't know who started the practice. I suspect it's like a good recipe, passed down from family to family. The idea is very simple: As you receive Christmas cards, put them in a basket in the middle of the dinner table or in another prominent family location. When you are ready to have Christmas card prayer time, take the cards out one by one and say a simple prayer or blessing for the family that sent it. The blessing can be plain ("God bless the Martinez family") or tailored ("God bless the Chen family, as Anna goes to college and Peter starts his new job"). Take added time to tell stories about the families who sent them, read the letters that have been included, and pray God's blessing upon the entire family. At the end of the Christmas season, before recycling the cards, take one last opportunity to flip through them, naming the recipients and giving thanks to God for their lives. Say a prayer at the end of your time together:

God, thank you so much for the families who have sent us these cards. Please bless each one throughout the year. May they feel the presence of your Spirit, even now as we pray. Amen.

Creative Night In

Imagination, beauty, and creativity are all spiritual practices that can easily go by the wayside during a busy Advent season. Make it a special point to do something creative as a family without a lot of pressure. Gather together all of the art supplies in your house: paper, glue, markers, crayons, and so forth, and get everyone together for a creative evening in. Make the evening as low-stress as possible by having no rules. Each person is allowed to create whatever they wish, Advent-related or no. You'll find surprising and delightful creations spring forth!

Las Novenas

In Colombia, where my husband, Elias, is from, many people celebrate "Las Novenas," which is nine days of celebrations from December 16 to December 24. Though a complicated liturgy and booklets are used in the celebrations in Colombia, this very simple family version has a nine-part prayer. The prayer is meant to be read every day for nine days. The template, for those who would like to write their own is as follows:

Part 1: Opening

Part 2: for Mary

Part 3: for Joseph

Part 4: for the baby Jesus

Part 5: for the wise men

Part 6: for the angels

Part 7: for today

Part 8: for joys

Part 9: closing

Here's an example of a nine-part "novena" prayer:

God, we give you thanks for this day, and every day, and during these nine days we remember:

Mary, the mother of Jesus, who was an example of faith and courage;

Joseph, Jesus' earthly father, who was an example of loyalty and strength;

The Baby Jesus, who was God, born as a tiny baby;

The wise men, who came bringing gifts to the new baby;

And the heavenly angels whose song filled the night sky.

Today we thank you for these things.

We celebrate the joys in our lives.

With hope and peace, joy and love, we pray, Amen.

You can write the prayer all at once and read it every day for nine days, or you can take your time and add one line each day for nine days until you have included all of the parts.

Nature Walk

Depending on where you live, this one might require lots of bundling up, but fresh air in the winter is needed more than ever when we're cooped up inside. Plan to take a walk outside, either in your neighborhood or in a forest, and notice the things around you that remind you of Advent and Christmas, whether it's snow, or pine needles, or red berries of some kind. Breathe in fresh air and give thanks to God for the gift of creation. You can even say together as a family, "Thank you, God, for the gift of creation. Help us to enjoy this walk around your world." Perhaps you will choose to take some of the pine needles as a bed for baby Jesus, or some twigs to make an acts of kindness tree. Every piece of connection to the world around you is a blessing.

Hot Chocolate Gratitude Party

One of the most popular practices from my first book *Faithful Families: Creating Sacred Moments at Home* is also one of the simplest. Called "Gratitude Café," the practice involves getting everyone's favorite beverages and sitting together sharing the things for which the family is grateful.

This Christmas practice is an even simpler variation on this theme. Fix steaming mugs of hot chocolate and take turns practicing gratitude while the chocolate cools.

Each person shares their gratitude until everyone has had a turn. End by saying, "Thank you, God, for these gifts. Amen."

A Christmas Story per Day

This is one of those ideas I've seen passed around the internet, and I'm not sure where it came from originally. My family has done this for a couple of years and loved it.

Buy or borrow 24 picture books about the season of Advent, Christmas, or winter; wrap them all up; and number them 1–24. Every evening from December 1 to Christmas Eve, unwrap a book and read together. My children have loved the anticipation and excitement of opening the books, even though they are books they have long known and loved.

The joy of the practice is in the surprise and the togetherness, not in the books, so don't worry too much if you don't have enough Christmas-themed books. Wrap up any book around your house, and you'll find the practice to be just as meaningful and fun as if it were a Christmas book.

Prayers
and Blessings for Family Time

Before a Meal with Family

Thank you, God, for the company of family, the gift of nourishing food, and time to enjoy family and food together. Amen.

When Family Comes to Town

Thank you, God, for the gift of family. May our family feel welcome in our home while they are here. Let us enjoy our time together and show our love to one another. Help us to cherish the moments of togetherness and live in the present moment.

Gratitude for Many Blessings/Advent Gratitude

During Advent, we say, "Thank you."

Thank you, God, for time together.

Thank you, God, for special food.

Thank you, God, for special moments.

Thank you, God, for gifts.

Thank you, God, for each new day.

For Family and Friends Far Away

God, we send blessings and love to friends and family far away:

May they feel our love.

May they know we miss them.

May they be happy and at peace.

May their Advent and Christmas be full of hope and peace, love and joy.

Chapter 4: Giving

During Advent and Christmas we often say, "'Tis better to give than to receive," but how do we model the value of giving as a family? How does our spiritual practice inform our relationship to gifts and giving? This chapter offers a variety of practices and prayers that focus on giving to others, being altruistic, and looking outside of ourselves. The focus is less on gifts that can be bought in a store and more on gifts of the heart. As we turn our attention to these things, the billion-dollar consumer-driven business of Christmas fades into the background, and the important things—those which cannot be bought—become the priority. Even a thoughtfully worded letter makes a lovely gift. These giving practices are centered in the belief that the most important part of gift giving is the intention behind the gift: to show love and gratitude to the recipient. The most valuable gifts are given with love.

Spiritual Practices
for Giving

Homemade Gift Party

Give the gift of your own creativity and time. Spend an evening making gifts together as a family, either to give to one another or to give to other family and friends. The sky's the limit as far as what kinds of gifts you choose to make. Gifts could be homemade edible treats such as cookies or candies, or they could arts and crafts–based. Here are five simple homemade gifts to make with simple materials:

- **Bookmark:** Cut out watercolor paper or construction paper into bookmarks. Color or paint. Punch a hole in the top for ribbon or yarn.

- **Picture frame:** Paint a plain frame, or use craft sticks to make a simple frame.

- **Flower pot:** Terracotta flower pots are easy to paint with acrylic paint. Give the pots by themselves or with a plant inside.

- **Pillow case:** Use fabric markers to write or draw on pillowcases. Be sure to put cardboard or poster board in the middle to keep the marker from bleeding through.

- **Ornament:** Decorate pinecones by painting, using glue and glitter, or adding ribbon for a unique ornament using something found in nature.

Check out a book at the library or search the internet for even more ideas. The process of making the gifts can be just as fun as giving them. Begin your homemade gift party by remembering the intention behind the gift—to show love and appreciation to the recipient.

Give a Gift to Baby Jesus

Nativity scenes, or crèches, are a lovely way to visualize the narrative of Christ's birth. Whether they're made of wood or porcelain, glass or plastic, each tells the story with the figures of Mary, Joseph, and the baby Jesus. Some nativity scenes include other characters such as shepherds, wise men, and animals, whereas others are the holy family alone in a manger. This practice works with whatever nativity scene you happen to have at home.

To make the nativity scene come alive, consider adding something to the scene. What could you bring from your home or outside to add to the scene? Some ideas for things to add are:

- Straw or hay for the manger.
- Dirt or soil under the feet of the figures (don't be afraid to get messy!).
- Glitter or sparkles to represent the Spirit.
- Twinkle lights or candles.
- Flowers (real or artificial).

What is added to the nativity scene matters less than the action of adding something to the scene and talking about it. Bringing something new to the scene each year will help make the scene less static and formal and breathe life and fresh air into it.

Year-Round Christmas Gift

Being able to give generously to a charity at Christmastime is a joy and pleasure for the whole family and a blessing for the charity who will receive the gift. Choose a charity at the beginning of the year and put out a large jar to collect loose change and bills for the year. Then, in the middle of December, take all the money to the bank and write one check to the organization. Include a note explaining that your family collected funds all year and thought and prayed for their good work all year. Keep a sign or a note next to the jar explaining what the funds are for, and visitors to your home will have the opportunity to learn about the charity you're supporting as well. Remember that the size of the gift is not as important as the dedication and thought behind the giving.

The Gifts All Around

Help your family think about how the things we use every day can be gifts. Read this short meditation:

When you take a drink of clean water from the water fountain at school, that's a gift. When you take a deep breath and fill your lungs with fresh air for your body, that's a gift. When you put on clean socks or shoes that fit your feet, that's a gift. When you give or receive a hug from someone you love, that's a gift. There are gifts all around us, every day. At Christmastime, there is a lot of talk about gifts, but the important thing to know is that gifts don't need to be bought in a store and wrapped in a bow. When you are thankful for the things you have, you have all of the gifts you could ever want or need.

After reading it aloud, take some time to identify the gifts all around you. Make a list. One way to do this practice is as a one-time activity where you gather together as a family and see how many gifts you can think of that are hiding in plain sight. Another way to do this is to put a piece of paper on the wall titled "The Gifts All Around" and add to the list throughout the season.

The Gift of You

At Christmastime there are a lot of commercials and signs trying to get people to buy new things. Even though the things are supposed to be gifts to give other people, it can still feel hard to decide what to buy our friends and family. We might wonder, *What if our friends don't like what we give?* or, *What if they already have one?* The good news is this: The people who love you the most want one thing—to be with you as your friend or family member. They already have what they want from you. They have you. So if you want to give your friends and family something really special, give them something that only you can give: a drawing, or a letter, or something else you made all yourself. They will love it so much because it can't be bought in a store.

What is a gift that only you can give? Think about the answer and share it with your family.

The Story of Saint Nicholas, the Secret Giver

You've probably heard the song "Jolly Old Saint Nicholas," about the man who comes down the chimney and puts presents in stockings, but have you heard about Saint Nicholas, the man who lived in modern-day Turkey 250 years after Jesus? Not a lot is known about him, but many people said that he was a very generous gift-giver and that he liked to give his gifts in secret. One story says that there was a time when Saint Nicholas wanted to help three people, but he didn't want them to know. He put gold coins in three bags and, at night, threw them through the window of the house where the three people lived. What a surprise the people must have had when they opened the bags with gold! The Bible says, "But when you give...do not let your left hand know what your right hand is doing" (Matthew 6:3). This is another way of saying that some gifts should be given anonymously, without calling attention to the gift. Do you know anyone who might benefit from an anonymous gift? How could you give them a surprise gift, without anyone knowing it was you who gave the gift?

Kindness Rocks

The Kindness Rocks Project™ was started by one person, Megan Murphy, in 2015 when she painted a rock with the words "You've got this" and left it on the beach for someone else to find. Many other people have picked up on this trend and have left painted rocks around for others to find and collect. The project has grown in popularity, and you can find detailed instructions on the movement's website (https://www.thekindnessrocksproject.com/). Kindness Rocks are a great activity for home and church because they require such few materials (rocks and paint!), and they can be done anytime and anywhere. Take some time to spread some kindness during the Advent and Christmas season.

Prayers
for Giving

As We Seek to Serve Others

As we seek to serve others, May we use our eyes to see those who are in need. May we use our ears to hear those who are crying out for help. May we use our mouths to speak up against the wrongs of the world. May our Advent time be focused on others and not ourselves.

For Generosity

To be generous means to give as much as we are able, trusting that we have enough to share. God, please help us to be generous this season and always.

Gratitude for Receiving a Gift

God, thank you for this gift, and for the person who gave it to me. Amen.

Chapter 5: Telling the Story

The story of Christ's birth has been passed down for generations in many different ways. It's the story that anchors us to the season, gives it meaning, and reminds us what we're celebrating. This chapter tells the story of Christ's birth through a short series of reflections. Read these around the dinner table in the days leading up to Christmas, as bedtime reflections, or at any other time you'd like to bring a bit of the wondrous story into your daily routine. Each reflection gives a short opening verse or verses, a scripture passage to read, a short reflection, and questions for discussion. If you are short on time, you can use the opening verse to anchor your reflection and discussion, but if time allows, consider looking up the entire passage in a children's Bible (or online) and reading it together as a family.

These stories have been passed down, from generation to generation. The reflections aren't "one size fits all." I've tried to write them in a way that reaches the broadest audience possible, but you know your family best. If a particular reflection seems "too young" or "too old" for your group, feel free to skip it, or tailor it as you can to meet the needs in your family. Follow where children lead. Ask questions with them and wonder right alongside them. Each passing year brings new insight to these stories, which are simultaneously ancient and fresh.

Jesus' Family Tree

Read together as a family: *Matthew 1:1–6. An account of the genealogy of Jesus the Messiah, the son of David, the son of Abraham. Abraham was the father of Isaac, and Isaac the father of Jacob, and Jacob the father of Judah and his brothers, and Judah the father of Perez and Zerah by Tamar, and Perez the father of Hezron, and Hezron the father of Aram, and Aram the father of Aminadab, and Aminadab the father of Nahshon, and Nahshon the father of Salmon, and Salmon the father of Boaz by Rahab, and Boaz the father of Obed by Ruth, and Obed the father of Jesse, and Jesse the father of King David.*

Reflection: Many people know their grandparents, and sometimes their great-grandparents or great-great grandparents, but what about knowing your great-great-great-great-great grandparents or even further back than that? The only way to know someone that far away from you in years is through what is called a *genealogy*. A genealogy is a record of ancestors going as far back as the record shows. Jesus' genealogy is written down two times in the Bible, and there are a variety of different biblical ancestors in each one. In Luke's genealogy, Jesus' ancestors go all the way back to God! The other genealogy in the Bible is Matthew's version. His version doesn't go as far back as God, but it still has the names of many important men and women in Jesus' family tree. One of the great things about genealogies is that they remind us of where we have come from. The things we do in our lifetime may be recorded and remembered by someone fifty or one hundred, or even five hundred years from now. As we learn more about the members of Jesus' family tree, we understand our faith stories better.

Talk about it: *What do you know about your family tree? What do you know about relatives who lived long ago?*

Joseph and the Angel

Read together as a family: *Matthew 1:20–21. [A]n angel of the Lord appeared to him [Joseph]...and said, "...you are to name him Jesus, for he will save his people from their sins."*

Reflection: Before Jesus was born, an angel came to Joseph, Jesus' father on earth. The angel talked to Joseph about many things, and one of them was what the baby should be called. The angel said that the baby should be named Jesus. The name Jesus (in Hebrew, *Yeshua*) comes from a word that means "to save" or "to rescue." A sin is anything that separates us from God's presence and love. The angel says that Jesus will save his people from their sins. It's right there in his name! It's wonderful to know that, even before he was born, God was preparing people to understand Jesus' special mission: to show people God's love by rescuing them from anything that separates them from God.

Talk about it: *Jesus' name is very special. What does his name mean to you? What do you know about the meaning of your own name?*

Mary's Song of Praise

Read together as a family: *Luke 1:46–50.*

And Mary said,
"My soul magnifies the Lord,
*   and my spirit rejoices in God my Savior,*
for he has looked with favor on the lowliness of his servant.
*   Surely, from now on all generations will call me blessed;*
for the Mighty One has done great things for me,
*   and holy is his name.*
His mercy is for those who fear him
*   from generation to generation."*

Reflection: When Mary found out that she was pregnant, she went to visit her cousin, Elizabeth, who was also expecting a baby. When the two met each other, Elizabeth's baby, John, jumped for joy! Mary was so happy that she sang a song of praise to God. We just read the beginning of this song, but it continues in Luke chapter 1. The song is called the "Magnificat," which is the first word of the song in Latin. Mary's song of joy continues on to talk about Jesus' important mission to take care of the poor and needy and lift them up. Rich people who do not care about the poor will be punished, the song says. Mary's song reminds us that Jesus' purpose on earth is to take care of those who are vulnerable and needy.

Talk about it: *How does Mary's song help us to understand what Jesus' ministry would be? Why does Mary's soul magnify God?*

Shepherds

Read together as a family: *Luke 2:8–14. In that region there were shepherds living in the fields, keeping watch over their flock by night. Then an angel of the Lord stood before them, and the glory of the Lord shone around them, and they were terrified. But the angel said to them, "Do not be afraid; for see—I am bringing you good news of great joy for all the people: to you is born this day in the city of David a Savior, who is the Messiah, the Lord. This will be a sign for you: you will find a child wrapped in bands of cloth and lying in a manger." And suddenly there was with the angel a multitude of the heavenly host, praising God and saying, "Glory to God in the highest heaven, and on earth peace among those whom he favors!"*

Reflection: God chose shepherds to be the very first people to hear the good news about the birth of the baby Jesus. The shepherds were watching their sheep and protecting them from danger, just like they did on any other night. All of a sudden, they heard a message from angels telling them not to be afraid, and giving them instructions for seeing the baby Jesus. They followed the directions and went to meet the baby. What an amazing night that must have been. The story of the shepherds reminds us that God can surprise us and meet us anytime with good news.

Talk about it: *What do you think it felt like to receive such an exciting message and good news? Why do you think the angel said, "Do not be afraid"?*

No Room in the Inn

Read together as a family: *Luke 2:1–7. In those days a decree went out from Emperor Augustus that all the world should be registered. This was the first registration and was taken while Quirinius was governor of Syria. All went to their own towns to be registered. Joseph also went from the town of Nazareth in Galilee to Judea, to the city of David called Bethlehem, because he was descended from the house and family of David. He went to be registered with Mary, to whom he was engaged and who was expecting a child. While they were there, the time came for her to deliver her child. And she gave birth to her firstborn son and wrapped him in bands of cloth, and laid him in a manger, because there was no place for them in the inn.*

Reflection: When Mary and Joseph were looking for a place for the baby Jesus to be born, the Bible says there was no room for them in the inn. Because of this, they had to go to a stable where there were animals and a manger for the baby Jesus to be born. Can you imagine it? No room for Jesus! And yet, even though there was no room in the inn, there was still room for him in the stable. Jesus' birth reminds us that there is always room for God to do something miraculous, even if it's not what we expect.

Talk about it: *Have you ever seen God do something unexpected? What was it?*

Immanuel

Read Together as a family: *Isaiah 7:14. Therefore the Lord himself will give you a sign. Look, the young woman is with child and shall bear a son, and shall name him Immanuel.*

Reflection: In the Bible we learn that another thing Jesus will be called is *Immanuel.* Immanuel means "God with us." One of the things that Jesus tells us in the Bible is that he has all of the same powers God has. This includes being able to be near to us all the time, whenever we call. This is a mystery, because we can't see Jesus anymore. Still, we know he is present with us whenever we need him. If we are lost or lonely, scared or tired, we can always call on Jesus, *Immanuel,* to be with us. Psalm 139:7 says, *"Where can I go from your spirit? Or where can I flee from your presence?"* The answer is that there is *nowhere* we can go where God and Jesus are not present. They are always there, together with the Holy Spirit. We can close our eyes and feel God's presence and power anytime we need it. God is with us all the time and everywhere.

Talk about it: *What does the word* Immanuel *mean to you?*

God's Love Is for All

Read together as a family: *Luke 2:9-12. Then an angel of the Lord stood before them, and the glory of the Lord shone around them, and they were terrified. But the angel said to them, "Do not be afraid; for see—I am bringing you good news of great joy for all the people: to you is born this day in the city of David a Savior, who is the Messiah, the Lord. This will be a sign for you: you will find a child wrapped in bands of cloth and lying in a manger."*

Reflection: When Jesus was born, the angel said, *"I am bringing you good news of great joy for all the people"* (Luke 2:10b). God's love is for all! When Jesus came into the world, his message was inclusive, which means "for everyone." There is nobody in the whole world who is outside of God's love. Sometimes people feel left out, or ignored, or not important. When that happens, it's our job as followers of Jesus to make sure they feel included and special. We can reach out with words or actions to help make sure they know the good news: God's love is for all!

Talk about it: *Who do you know that needs to hear the good news that God's love is for all? What can you say or do to share that good news?*

Go Tell It on the Mountain

Read together as a family: *Matthew 28:16–20. Now the eleven disciples went to Galilee, to the mountain to which Jesus had directed them. When they saw him, they worshiped him; but some doubted. And Jesus came and said to them, "All authority in heaven and on earth has been given to me. Go therefore and make disciples of all nations, baptizing them in the name of the Father and of the Son and of the Holy Spirit, and teaching them to obey everything that I have commanded you. And remember, I am with you always, to the end of the age."*

Reflection: The famous Christmas song says, "Go tell it on the mountain, over the hills and everywhere. Go, tell it on the mountain that Jesus Christ is born!" The message of this song is the message of *evangelism*, which means "sharing the good news." Sharing the good news that Jesus is born is one of the joys of following Jesus. We have the opportunity to share the hope, peace, joy, and love of Jesus with one another. We can share the good news of Jesus with our actions. Every time we do something kind and loving for another person, we are sharing the good news of Jesus. Other times, we might want to share the good news with our words by telling someone about this good news. Whether it is in words or actions, we have the opportunity to share about Jesus' birth and what it means for us.

Talk about it: *How will you share the good news of Jesus' birth? Would you rather share with words or with actions? Why?*

The X in X-Mas

Read together as a family: *Luke 2:25–28a. Now there was a man in Jerusalem whose name was Simeon; this man was righteous and devout, looking forward to the consolation of Israel, and the Holy Spirit rested on him. It had been revealed to him by the Holy Spirit that he would not see death before he had seen the Lord's Messiah. Guided by the Spirit, Simeon came into the temple; and when the parents brought in the child Jesus, to do for him what was customary under the law, Simeon took him in his arms and praised God.*

Reflection: Have you ever heard Jesus referred to as Jesus *Christ*? "Christ" isn't Jesus' last name. Instead, it's his title, which means "Messiah" or "Savior." When we say Jesus Christ, we are saying that Jesus is our Savior. In Greek, the language the New Testament was written in, *Christ,* is spelled like this: Χριστός. Do you notice the first letter? It's an "X." When people replace the word Christ with an "X," they're not trying to remove Christ from Christmas; they're just making a shortcut. The X is a symbol for Jesus Christ that has been used by people since the year 1021. That's a long time! Simeon, whose story we just read, was one of the first people who noticed Jesus as the savior of all. We follow in Simeon's footsteps every time we recognize Jesus as Jesus the Christ.

Talk about it: *If someone says that "X-mas" is a way to take Christ out of Christmas, what would you say? What does it mean to say Jesus is our Savior?*

The Light of the World

Read together as a family: *John 1:1–5. In the beginning was the Word, and the Word was with God, and the Word was God. He was in the beginning with God. All things came into being through him, and without him not one thing came into being. What has come into being in him was life, and the life was the light of all people. The light shines in the darkness, and the darkness did not overcome it.*

Reflection: Once, I was in a very dark, deep cave where there was no sunlight at all. Unlike being in a room that is *mostly* dark, but with a tiny amount of light from stars or the sun or the moon, this cave was complete darkness. If I put my hand in front of my face, I could not even see it. Then, the cave guide lit a single match. Everything in the whole cave was visible and clear by the light of that one small light.

At Christmastime we remember that Jesus came to earth to bring light to the world. It says this in the book of John, chapter 1: "What has come into being in him [Jesus] was life, and the life was the light of all people" (John 1:3b–4). This verse reminds us that even in the darkest night, Jesus brings us the light we can use to see the rest of the world. The light of Jesus shines brightly when things are dark or difficult.

Talk about it: *When have you been in a place when there wasn't enough light to see?*

Chapter 6: Advent Values

In many churches, the four weeks of Advent are marked by a discussion on four specific values: hope, peace, joy, and love. Traditionally, one value is discussed each week and is marked by the lighting of candles which correspond with the values. (See page 10 for a family Advent lighting tradition that mirrors the church one.) For a deeper dive into the Advent values, this chapter offers reflections and prayers to lead you. Use them as inspiration for your own family (or ministry) discussions on these Advent values. If you like, you can focus on one of the values each week as the church does, or you can cycle through the values in a less systematic way, as you feel led and interested. In the "thinking about" sections, please use my reflections in any way that is helpful to you. Use them to get your own juices flowing on the Advent values, read them aloud to your family or congregation, or allow them to be a personal guide for you through the Advent values.

Reflecting
on the Advent Values

Advent Hope

Thinking about hope: The first week of Advent is the week of hope. In my house, we speak both Spanish and English. Sometimes it's fun to see how certain words in one language will help us to understand words in the other language. One example of this is the word *esperar*, which means "to wait." *Esperar* also means "to hope." So, in Spanish, hoping and waiting are the same word. This is very similar to how the Bible talks about hoping and waiting. Romans 8:25 says, "But if we hope for what we do not see, we wait for it with patience." So having hope might also mean having patience. I wonder if that's because the things we hope for don't always come to us right away. What connections can you make between waiting and hoping that make sense in your family or church context? Perhaps there's something specific your family is hoping for or waiting for. Use the verse in Romans 8:25 to get your family conversation going.

Questions to guide your family discussion: *What does it feel like to wait? I wonder what hoping feels like.*

Family activities to explore hope:

- Draw a picture of the things you hope for.
- Fill a box with your hopes and dreams. Keep your box private or share with your family members.
- Planting seeds can be a symbol of hope, because it takes a long time for them to grow. Plant some seeds and watch them grow. If it's too cold to plant seeds now, make a plan to plant later.

Advent Peace

Thinking about peace: The second week of Advent is the week of peace. Peace is the absence of conflict and fighting, a sense of unity, calm, and togetherness. Peace can be felt within one person's heart, within a family, within a community, or even between countries in the world. Peace starts from within and then radiates outward. People who work toward peace in the world are called peacemakers. Jesus said, "Blessed are the peacemakers, for they will be called children of God" (Matthew 5:9). To be a peacemaker in the world, start with inner peace. Many people say that inner peace is as close as breathing. You can try this by closing your eyes and breathing in and out, in and out. Breathe in and count to four. Breathe out and count to eight. Try this a few times and see if you feel more peaceful.

Questions to guide your family discussion: *How does peace within your own heart help to create peace in the whole world? I wonder what peace feels like. I wonder how you share that peace with others.*

Things to do:

- Draw a picture of what peace means to you.
- Write a letter to someone you think is a peacemaker and thank them for their work.
- Look in magazines for pictures that seem peaceful or calming. Make them into a collage as a family.

Advent Joy

Thinking about joy: The third week of Advent is the week of joy. One of the most widely sung Christmas carols starts like this: "Joy to the world, the Lord is come!" What does it mean? Does it mean that because Jesus has come into the world, everyone will be happy, all of the time? I don't think so. Happiness is an emotion that we have when things are going well around us. It's wonderful to be happy. And yet, it's not likely that we will be happy all the time. Joy, even though it is often used to mean "happy," is not exactly the same. Joy is something that is not dependent on circumstances and is felt deep within one's heart. A person can be having difficult or sad circumstances and still feel a sense of joy within their heart. Does that sound confusing? If it's hard to grasp, just think about this: Jesus came into a world where there are all kinds of emotions—happiness, sadness, anger and loneliness, just to name a few. Even though all these emotions still exist, we can have joy that God is with us through them all.

Questions to guide your family discussion: *Do you think there is a difference between happiness and joy? How would you describe it? I wonder what joy feels like.*

Things to do:

- Draw a picture of something that brings you great joy.
- Smile at others when you see them. See if they smile back!
- Spend some time together as a family and share in joy together: bake cookies, play a game, or read a story.

Advent Love

Thinking about love: The fourth week of Advent is the week of love. Love is one of the most important things we can offer to another human being. In the Bible, 1 Corinthians chapter 13 tells a bit about some of the characteristics of love: love is patient and kind, and not arrogant or rude. Jesus says the most important thing we can do as human beings is love God, our neighbor, and ourselves. When we love others, we treat them as we would want to be treated, remembering always to be caring and kind. Jesus came into the world to show us how to love one another. As we learn more about Jesus, we learn more about how to love everyone in the world, just as he did.

Questions to guide your family discussion: *How can we show love to our neighbors during Advent? Who needs to know and feel our love most of all?*

Things to do:

- Think of something kind to do for someone who needs to feel love today.
- Draw a picture of what God's love means to you.
- Learn about sending love to others through a loving-kindness meditation.

Prayers
for the Advent Values

For Hope

To hope is to wait for something.

Hoping and waiting are the same.

   When we hope, we wait.

   When we wait, we hope.

May God be with us as we wait and hope

for Jesus.

For Peace

We can have peace every time we take a break.

We breathe in deep.

We can have peace every time we slow down.

We notice the world around us.

We can have peace every time we are quiet before God.

Thank you, God, for peace.

For Peace on Earth

Peace on Earth begins in our hearts, or between two people.

> We pray for peace in our families.

> We pray for peace in our homes.

> We pray for peace between all.

Let peace for the world begin in our hearts.

No peaceful act is too small to start changing the world.

For Joy

Joy is a smile that begins deep within. It rises and rises. We smile and laugh. To have joy means to be happy and to have everything we need. Thank you, God, for joy.

For Love

God, you ask us to love you.

Please help us to love you more every day.

God, you ask us to love our neighbors.

Please help us to love our neighbors more every day.

God, you ask us to love you and love our neighbors.

Help us to do both of those things,

> more and more each day.

By loving God, we love our neighbors.

By loving our neighbors, we love God.

For Our Neighbors and Friends

God, as we learn the Advent values of

hope, peace, joy, and love,

May we not keep them to ourselves.

May we share them with our friends and neighbors,

that our world might become

more hopeful,

more peaceful,

more joyful,

and

more loving.

Let me do my part to create this kind of world, today and every day.

Amen.

Chapter 7: Difficult Moments

Not all of the moments in Advent and Christmas are full of joy and contentment. In fact, sometimes the season can cause tough times to rise to the surface. The season itself can cause stress because of the added activities and family time. Sometimes we miss those who can't be present with us during the season because of loss or distance.

Sadness and joy exist together in family life. Too often families send the message (either implicitly or explicitly) that this is a season of joy, so children need to be happy and grateful. This chapter will guide you through some of the more challenging moments in the season so that you can honor them, creating space for all of the emotions we go through as human beings.

Spiritual Practices
for Difficult Moments

Stars in the Sky, Prayer Requests

Make a starry sky throughout Advent with all of your prayer requests. Here's how to do it:

Find a large piece of black or dark blue poster board or butcher paper and hang it up in a central location in the house. Cut out a number of white paper stars and put in a basket. Every time there is a joy or a concern, write it on a paper star and attach it to the sky. As Advent progresses, you'll have a sky full of joys and concerns that can serve as a visual reminder of the season's joys and concerns.

The Longest Night/Solstice—Marking Grief or Sadness

For those who live in the Northern Hemisphere, the longest night and shortest day falls between December 20 and December 22. The longest night is also called the winter solstice. If your family is feeling down for any reason or experiencing grief, the winter solstice is a good time to name that hard time or grief, mark it, and remember that subsequent days will be getting longer. The longest night doesn't last forever; the days eventually get longer and brighter.

All you need for this practice is a candle and the words below. Gather everyone around a table with the candle and say,

"Today, on this longest night, we remember that even though there is a lot of joy during the Advent season, sometimes there is sorrow, too. We light a candle for [name the reason you've decided to have a longest night ceremony]. We take a moment to remember that, though the nights can feel long and dark sometimes, brighter and longer days are coming soon. Let's pray together. *[Read the longest night prayer or any other prayer you like."]*

Longest Night Prayer

God, this candle reminds us that there is light, even in the longest night. We thank you for the opportunity to name the things that are difficult for us this season, and for the hope we have as the sun shines more and more each day. Help us to be near to one another and to you as we lift up our prayers on this day.

You can close your longest night moment by extinguishing the candle and saying, "Peace to our family and to our hearts. May we trust in the light that is to come. Peace, peace. Amen." After the ceremony, do something quiet together, enjoying one another's quiet presence. Snuggle together and watch a movie, or go for a drive to enjoy the Christmas lights around town. Remember that sadness and joy can exist together.

Prayers
for Difficult Moments

When Family Leaves

God, we thank you for the gift of family and for the gift of a visit.

As _____ leave to go home, we offer up our prayers:

We thank you for the good times we had together.

We look forward to seeing them again soon.

We ask you to bless them and bless us as we are apart.

When Things Get Too Busy

When things get too busy and it seems as if we have no time, we pause.

We breathe in.

We breathe out.

We give thanks.

Help us to look for moments of peace and calm in the middle of all the busy moments.

For a Difficult Time

When our family is going through a difficult time,

> We turn to each other.

> We turn to God.

> We ask for peace.

Help us, God, to have peace in good times
and in difficult times.

When Someone Is in the Hospital

God, we pray for _____, who is in the hospital today.

> May your Spirit bring peace and comfort.

> May your Spirit bring rest and company.

> May your Spirit bring light and wholeness.

For Those Who Are Lonely

For those who are alone:

> May they not feel lonely this day.

> May they know we are thinking them.

> And may they feel the Spirit, who is never far away.

When We Are Grieving

God, this season is hard because we miss [Name], who isn't here with us. Let us remember that it's okay to be sad. It is okay to miss them. It is okay to grieve. It is also okay to be happy and celebrate, knowing that things are different without our loved one. Meet us where we are, whatever we are feeling, and help us to have peace within. Amen.

When We Miss Someone

As we gather together, we realize that someone is missing.

We miss _____ today and wish they were here.

Memories of them make us happy.

We think of them with joy in our hearts.

We wish them peace where they are, and we pray that they are well.

When Family Is Far Away

God, we send blessings and love to friends and family far away:

> May they feel our love.
>
> May they know we miss them.
>
> May they be happy and at peace.
>
> May their Advent and Christmas be full of hope and peace, love and joy.

Amen.

Chapter 8: Christmas Eve and Christmas Day

December 24 and 25 are not important dates, biblically speaking. It's only because of church tradition that we celebrate the birth of Christ on these days. Even so, they are two of the most sacred days in the Christian liturgical rhythm. The practices in this chapter are small, glittering moments of tradition, sprinkled into your busy Christmas Eve and Christmas Day. The practices in this chapter don't necessarily need to happen on the twenty-fourth or twenty-fifth. If your Christmas Eve and Christmas Day are already jam-packed, pull these traditions out for a different day in the season. Merry, Merry!

Spiritual Practices
for Christmas Eve and Christmas Day

Christmas Eve Candle

Christmas Eve can be a very busy day, so here's a practice that is meaningful but doesn't take up much time. It is inspired by something from my own childhood: Every year when we took out the Christmas decorations, I remember one very large pillar candle. When the candle was unwrapped, my mom would explain that she and my dad bought it together on their honeymoon. They figured that if they burned it for just few hours every Christmas Eve, it would last for many years.

You can borrow this idea and have a special candle (or candleholder) that is just for Christmas Eve. As you light it say these special words: *On this Christmas Eve night, we remember Jesus is the light of the world. The light shines in our hearts and in our family.*

Silent Night Star Walk

There is something magical about going for a walk outside in the crisp, cool night air. It's a reminder that nature isn't revealed just by the light of day. A nighttime walk has a certain mystery and beauty to it. Depending on where you live, you may need to bundle up quite a bit for your silent night star walk. As you walk, look up at the stars and consider the majesty and beauty of God. After the walk, ask one another, "What did you see that reminded you of the beauty and majesty of God?"

Birthday Party for Jesus

Sometimes, in the midst of the Advent and Christmas season, we forget that it's a birthday celebration. Have fun remembering this by having a birthday party for Jesus! Decorate the house with streamers and balloons. Bake a cake. Sing "Happy Birthday." Give gifts of baby food or diapers to a food pantry as a present for the baby Jesus. Your birthday party can be as simple or as complicated as you choose. Perhaps you'll choose only one element of the party, such as the cake or the presents. Even a small reminder turns the focus from those gathered to the baby Jesus.

Reading the Christmas Story

The simplest practices can have profound impact over time. How often have you read a passage from the Bible out loud with your family? For some families, this is a weekly or even daily practice, but for many others, hearing the Bible read out loud is a practice reserved for church. Find some time to read the Christmas story on Christmas Eve or Christmas Day. It won't take long, and the impact will be profound. I recommend reading Luke's version Luke 2:1–20). You can print out several copies and take turns reading different verses, or one person can read all of the verses. Let the story speak for itself.

Ornament Stories

This is another simple practice that your family will remember for years to come. Ask each family member to find an ornament on the tree that has a special story. Take turns showing the ornament and telling what is meaningful to you about the ornament. If you have guests coming to your house for Christmas Eve or Christmas Day, ask them, in advance, to bring a special ornament with them so they'll also have a story to share. This is an activity that also works well over a video call to include those who are far away.

Prayers
for Christmas Eve and Christmas Day

Christmas Eve

On this holy night we remember the angels who said, "Do not fear." On this holy night we remember the shepherds who bowed down before the baby. On this holy night we remember Mary and Joseph, who had faith in God. On this holy night we remember Jesus, who came to save us. On this holy night we remember God is with us. Amen.

Christmas Eve, Before Bed

Goodnight, everyone, and peace.

We are watching and waiting and hoping
     for Christmas Day.

Before it arrives, we close our eyes and sleep.

Goodnight, everyone, and peace.

Thank you, God, for being with us when we sleep.

Christmas Morning

We open our eyes with joy.

Christmas Day is here!

We are happy to love,

   happy to share,

   happy to be with one another.

We pray today will be a special and holy day!

For the Gift of Being Together

There is no greater gift than the gift of love.

When we are together, we share in God's love.

We celebrate Jesus; we celebrate life.

Thank you, God, for the most important things.

Christmas Day Is Over

Christmas Day is over, but the spirit of Christmas lives on.

Christmas Day is over, but God's love is with us, always.

Chapter 9: The 12 Days of Christmas and Epiphany

As a pastor, I really appreciate the time after Christmas Day is over and while the decorations are still up. There's a sense of peace and calm as many of the activities are over for the season, and yet there's still a holy feeling lingering in the air. The practices in this chapter are for that season after Christmas Day is over. Many of the practices in this chapter focus on Epiphany. For those who didn't grow up with that term, Epiphany is the celebration when the magi (or wise men) visited Jesus and brought him gifts of gold, frankincense, and myrrh. There are many ways to celebrate that important day in the church calendar as a family. After Christmas is over, let the season linger awhile before it's all put away for the next year.

Spiritual Practices
for the 12 Days of Christmas and Epiphany

The 12 Days of Christmas Togetherness Challenge

After December 25, many people seem eager to put the season away until next year. The very next day, December 26, is a day of half-off sales for Christmas-related items, and many a Christmas tree is already waiting for trash pickup. And yet, for thousands of years, the Christian church has understood Christmas as a season that *begins* on December 25. The 12 days of Christmas extend from December 25 until Epiphany, the day the wise men visit Jesus, on January 6.

Celebrate this tradition in your home by challenging your family to do something special together every day for the 12 days of Christmas. Whether it's visiting a museum or other attraction, playing a board game together, or having hot cocoa and talking about what you're grateful for, challenge yourselves to enjoy all 12 days of Christmas together as a family.

Add the Magi and the Star to the Nativity

Another activity is for those who have crèches or nativity scenes to use throughout the season. When you put out the scene at the beginning of Advent, hold back the three magi from the scene. If your scene has a removable star, hold it back as well. If you don't have a star, make one out of poster board or cardboard and paste it on the wall behind the scene. As you place them in your scene, you can say these words:

Star: We place this star in the sky to remind us of how the star guided the magi to the baby Jesus. The star shone brightly in the sky. May we also shine brightly as we share goodness and kindness with the world.

Magi: We place the magi in our scene to remember the three gifts they brought to the baby Jesus. Gold, which glitters and represents his royalty; frankincense which has a fragrant smell and represents his holiness; and myrrh, which is bitter and represents the bitterness of his last days. As the magi bring their gifts, may we remember to bring our gifts as well.

Epiphany Practice: Star Gifts

Many churches, including mine, have a practice of offering a "star gift" at the beginning of the year. Words to guide the year are written on stars and gathered in a basket, and then family members each draw a random star. Each person's word becomes a gift to guide them throughout the year. Replicate this practice at home and do the same thing. All you need to do is write 25 words on paper stars (or slips of paper) and have each person pull one out of a basket. Talk about how the word might guide you for the year to come. See how your star gift informs your life for the year to come. Here are 25 words you can use:

Hope	Joy	Peace	Love	Kindness
Faith	Goodness	Humility	Respect	Imagination
Wisdom	Friendship	Courage	Time	Rest
Comfort	Help	Gratitude	Giving	Family
Trust	Caring	Grace	Fun	Play

When my congregation does this exercise, I always remind them that the stars are supposed to be gifts, not "homework." As you pull your star out from the basket, imagine that the word it contains will be a gift to you for the year to come, not a call to have to work harder at something. See the ways the word comes into your life in surprising ways! Have fun.

Epiphany Practice: Chalking the Door

I first learned of the practice of "chalking the door" from my Episcopal friends. I have since learned that many Christians participate in this tradition, either on January 6 (Epiphany) or on January 5 (the Eve of Epiphany). For this practice, all you need is a piece of chalk and the words listed below. To chalk the door, simply write the first two numbers of the year and the letters C, M, and B. At the end, write the last two numbers in the year. Separate each item with a + or cross. For example, in 2021, the chalked door would look like this:

20 + C + M + B + 21

The letters in the middle have two meanings. First, they are the traditional names of the three magi who visited the baby Jesus: Caspar, Melchior, and Balthasar. These names are not recorded in scripture, nor does scripture say that there were exactly three magi, but these names have become an important part of church tradition. C, M, and B are also the first three letters of the phrase *Christus mansionem benedicat,* which means "May Christ bless this house." After you put the letters and numbers on the doorframe and explain what they mean, end with this simple blessing: *May Christ bless this home and all who live here. May Christ bless this home and all who visit here. May we all share the love of God, the grace of Christ, and the friendship of the Spirit. Amen.*

Epiphany Practice: Leaving Hay for Camels

Here's a fun practice that children in many other countries, particularly Latin American countries, enjoy doing. On the Eve of Epiphany, January 5, put some straw or hay in your shoes or in a small box under your bed for the camels of the wise men. As they pass by on their way to visit the baby Jesus, they will eat the straw and leave a small present or some chocolates in return. Have fun decorating the box before you fill it with the grass or straw. If you live in a place where it's hard to find fresh grass in the beginning of January, you can improvise by putting in carrots or lettuce or anything else you imagine a camel might eat. You can also say these special words: *O Holy Magi, as you go on your trip to see the baby Jesus, we remember you. Thank you for following the light of the star and for your faith. Amen.*

Have an Epiphany Party

An Epiphany party is a great way to spend time together and savor the last moments of the Christmas season in a fun way. Invite friends or family to your Epiphany party, or enjoy with just the people in your house. Things you might include in your Epiphany party:

- A special cake. Many cultures have special king cakes to celebrate Epiphany. In some traditions a bean or plastic baby is hidden in the cake. The one who finds it is the host of a second party.

- Do one (or more) of the other Epiphany practices listed in this book.

- Decorate with white lights or white paper stars.

- Read the story of the magi in Matthew 2:1–12.

- Make paper crowns and decorate them.

- Sing a song or hymn about light, stars, or the three kings.

Make your Epiphany party a treasured part of the season and create lasting memories. Your Epiphany party can be uniquely yours and is whatever you decide it will be. Have fun, use your imagination, and let your light shine!

Prayers
for the 12 Days of Christmas and Epiphany

A Prayer for the 12 Days of Christmas

Christmas Day is done, but the season of Christmas is just beginning.

> Twelve days to celebrate the season of Christmas.

> Twelve days to be together.

> Twelve days to be thankful.

> Twelve days to share the love of Jesus.

God, be with us through these twelve days, Amen.

A Prayer for New Year's Eve

As the clock turns from one year to the next,
we say thank you, God.

> Thank you for the year that has passed.

> Thank you for the year to come.

Each new year brings new joys and new concerns.
Make us ready for whatever will come this year, Amen.

A Prayer for New Year's Day

The year changes, but God's love stays the same.

We wonder what might happen this year.

No matter what this new year brings, one thing will be true:

God will be with us each and every day.

We start the new year with joy and hope.

Epiphany Prayer

The star in the sky showed the magi the way to the baby Jesus.

> The star was a guide.

> The star was a light.

> The star was a promise.

As we follow in the ways Jesus has taught us,

> God be our guide.

> God be our light.

> God be our promise.

Amen.

Chapter 10: Endings

After all of the preparation and excitement of Christmas, it seems to be over in a flash. Just as it's nice to ease into the season with deliberate preparation, creating a meaningful end to the season helps the transition between the Christmas season and the rest of the year. This chapter gently leads you through practices that help your family carry the spirit of Christmas through the rest of the year and set your family up for success next year.

Spiritual Practices for Ending the Season

Memory Box for the Year to Come

This practice, which was also in my first book *Faithful Families: Creating Sacred Moments at Home,* is one of those practices that takes a little bit of effort for a huge payoff later. Simply get a box or a jar, and fill it with memories from the year. Write down simple things and include the date: "We had blueberry pancakes for breakfast on March 3." You can also put ticket stubs, programs, and other memories from the year in the box or jar. Then next year, on New Year's Eve or New Year's Day, take turns pulling out memories from the box and enjoying them. You can recycle the memories or paste them into a scrapbook to enjoy for future years.

Unhanging the Greens

January can be a little bit of a letdown, as the Christmas season is over. For those who live where it's cold in winter, the days can be dark and grey, and the season has lost its sparkle. Take time to acknowledge the end of the season as you put everything away. Many churches have a celebration when they "hang the greens"; why not have a celebration to unhang them? Gather everyone together and reflect on the best parts of the Christmas season. What memories will you hold on to? What was your favorite part of the season? Talk about your memories from the season as you take the decorations down and put them away. Give thanks to God for the season and the gifts it brought. After you put everything away, notice how you feel. If you feel a sense of grief or loss at the changing of the season, take a moment to set up a new sacred space for the coming months. Find a table or corner of your house where you can put a few candles, a plant, or any other sacred symbol. Let that new space be a holy space for the coming months.

Preparing for Next Year

Sometimes, when I do something to prepare for the future, I like to think of it as giving my future self a gift. This practice is all about giving your future self a gift as you prepare for next year's Advent. As I mentioned in the introduction, one thing you can do is to pack this book in a box with your other Christmas decorations, so it's right there waiting for you next year when you need it. You can also gather and store together some of the supplies for practices you'll want to do the following year. If you're doing a Christmas story per day, for example, you can wrap up the books, number them, and put them away all ready to go. Put a Christmas tree blessing next to your ornaments, or make a list of supplies you'll need to find early in the season next year. This practice can be done individually or as a family. Your future self will thank you!

Thank You Note Party

Writing thank you notes is a lost art. I don't have my children write thank you notes as much as I wish I did. Make it fun by doing it all together and making a party out of it. At the end of the season, sit down and write notes together. For children who aren't old enough to write yet, let them draw pictures, or write down what they dictate to you. Include photos of your family enjoying the season together or enjoying specific gifts. Write "old-fashioned" pencil and paper notes, or create more modern versions such as video messages, text messages, emails with attachments, or social media messages. Whatever format you choose, the most important part is showing gratitude.

Looking Back and Looking Forward

January is a good time to take inventory of the year that has just passed as well as the year to come. Combine your year-end review with a look forward to the upcoming year in one family meeting. Use the following questions to guide you as you reflect.

Reflecting on the year that has just passed:

- What are three memories from last year that make you smile?
- What are three things you are grateful for that happened last year?
- Draw a picture of one happy memory from last year.

Reflecting on the year to come:

- What new thing would you like to do this year?
- What skill or habit would you like to work on this year? (What are your goals?)
- How can we show kindness to others in the year to come?

Share your answers to the questions on paper or out loud as a family. Take a video of your answers and let it be a digital time capsule for you to review the following year.

Advent All Year—Leaving Something as a Reminder

The message of Christmas is that God came to earth as a tiny baby to show the world just how much love God has for the world. This message isn't limited to the Christmas season; it's a message for every day of the year! To symbolize this powerful truth, choose one small decoration or item to leave out in your home as a reminder. Perhaps it will be one of the figures from the nativity set, or some other small item. You could even add a small paper sign that says, "Let's remember Christmas all year."

Another way to celebrate the message of Christmas all year is to have a "Christmas in July" celebration. In the middle of July, get out some Christmas music, read the story of Christ's birth, and share in the joy of Christmas, right in the middle of summer. It will be a wonderful surprise!

Prayers
for Ending the Season

When Family Leaves to Go Home

Though we can be separated from our family by miles, we are never separated in our hearts. Though we say goodbye to our family as they leave our home, we know we will soon say hello in a new way. Bless our family as they travel. May we remember the good times we had together. May we hold each other in our hearts. Amen.

When We Take the Decorations Down

We put the decorations up to remember a special season.

We take them down and remember this special time.

We put things away gently and look forward to taking them out again next year.

Next year they will be new again.

Next year they will be waiting for us.

Next year they will bring us joy and happiness.

A Prayer of Gratitude for the Season

Thank you, God, for the lessons of this season.

Thank you, God, for each special moment.

Thank you, God, for Christmas.

Carrying Christmas With Us All Year

The message of Christmas is for every day.

The message of Christmas is for every person.

God loves every person, every day.

This is the good news to remember, always.

Acknowledgments

Book production is an art and a science, and thanks is due to so many beautiful humans who have contributed to this little and lovely book. First and most importantly to Brad Lyons at Chalice Press for relentless encouragement and belief in my ideas when I didn't believe in them myself. To Gail Stobaugh and Tanya Campen for astute and insightful shepherding of this manuscript. To the rest of the Chalice Press team including Deborah Arca, Krista Schaeffer, Jim Stropnik, Judy Cullen, and Connie Wang for all of the book-making machinery and wizardry that made this book shine. To Paul: one should never judge a book by its cover, unless that cover is designed by you. You're three for three. To Jen, Caryn, Glenys, Dave, Wendy, Arianne, and Lee for beautiful endorsements: I'm humbled and honored.

To all of the parents, authors, and ministry leaders who continue to support my work and vision for progressive children's ministry: I write for you. Thank you for the privilege.

Final and deepest gratitude to my partner in life, Elias Cabarcas, for being rock-solid and weathering all the storms of life with me. You give me space to write and to be who I am. I love you.

Traci Smith